Find Out About...
Victorian Britain

48 Differentiated Key Stage 2 Non-Fiction Texts with Questions

Introduction

Find Out About Victorian Britain is a collection of twelve different topics explored at four different reading levels. It is aimed at the busy teacher who needs to accurately differentiate classroom work to make sure all pupils in their care are working towards their maximum potential. The Levels used match the English National Curriculum. The Level 2 texts have a passage to copy out with missing words to be found. The remaining texts have simple factual questions in Section A and more open-ended/ inferred questions in Section B. Section C suggests ideas for illustrating the work. All the pages have been printed 'Landscape' to make maximum use of the space on Interactive Whiteboards. Black and white images are used in the paper book; full colour images have been used in the e.book and download.

Topical Resources publishes a range of Educational Materials for use in Primary Schools and Pre-School Nurseries and Playgroups.

For the latest catalogue:
Tel 01772 863158
Fax 01772 866153
email: sales@topical-resources.co.uk
Visit our Website at:
www.topical-resources.co.uk

Copyright © Peter Bell
First Published April 2011
ISBN 978-1-907269-48-6

Illustrated by John Hutchinson, Art Works, Fairhaven, 69 Worden Lane, Leyland, Preston

Designed by Paul Sealey, PS3 Creative, 3 Wentworth Drive, Thornton, Lancashire

Printed in the UK for 'Topical Resources' by T. Snape and Co Ltd., Boltons Court, Preston, Lancashire

Contents

1 The Reign of Queen Victoria
   Level 2 2
   Level 3 3
   Level 4 4
   Level 5 5

2 Town and Country Life
   Level 2 6
   Level 3 7
   Level 4 8
   Level 5 9

3 Everyday Life in a Terraced Row
   Level 2 10
   Level 3 11
   Level 4 12
   Level 5 13

4 Everyday Life in a Wealthy Home
   Level 2 14
   Level 3 15
   Level 4 16
   Level 5 17

5 Children at Work
   Level 2 18
   Level 3 19
   Level 4 20
   Level 5 21

6 School for All
   Level 2 22
   Level 3 23
   Level 4 24
   Level 5 25

7 The Workhouse
   Level 2 26
   Level 3 27
   Level 4 28
   Level 5 29

8 New Inventions and the Great Exhibition
   Level 2 30
   Level 3 31
   Level 4 32
   Level 5 33

9 The Growth of the Railways
   Level 2 34
   Level 3 35
   Level 4 36
   Level 5 37

10 Bicycles, Buses, Ships and Cars
   Level 2 38
   Level 3 39
   Level 4 40
   Level 5 41

11 Victorian Fashion
   Level 2 42
   Level 3 43
   Level 4 44
   Level 5 45

12 The British Empire
   Level 2 46
   Level 3 47
   Level 4 48
   Level 5 49

The Reign of Queen Victoria

Victoria became Queen in 1837, when she was

18 years old. Victoria was crowned in 1838 at

Westminster Abbey. Queen Victoria fell in love

with her cousin Prince Albert. They were married

in 1840. She had four sons and five daughters.

In 1861 Prince Albert died. This made the Queen

very unhappy and for many years she only wore

black clothes. In 1887 Victoria had been queen for

50 years. A great party was held for her. Queen

Victoria died in 1901.

Copy this writing and fill in the gaps:

The Reign of Queen Victoria

When she was _____ years old Victoria became Queen.
She was crowned at _____ Abbey in 1838.
Queen Victoria fell in love with her _____ Prince Albert.
They were _____ in 1840. She had five daughters
and _____ sons. Prince _____ died in 1861. This
made the Queen very _____ and for many years she
only wore _____ clothes. Victoria had been queen for
_____ years in 1887. A great _____ was held for her.
Queen Victoria died in _____.

The Reign of Queen Victoria

Victoria became Queen in 1837, when she was 18 years old. The people of Britain were glad to have a young queen. Victoria was crowned in 1838 at Westminster Abbey.

Queen Victoria fell in love with her cousin Prince Albert. They were married in 1840. Between 1841 and 1857 she had nine children. She had four sons and five daughters. Albert helped her to run the country.

In 1861 Prince Albert died. This made the Queen very unhappy and for many years she only wore black clothes. She refused to live in London and instead, stayed in her country houses. This meant that the Queen was disliked by her people.

In 1887 Victoria had been queen for 50 years. A great party was held for her. Wearing a black dress, she was driven through the streets of London. The people cheered showing that they liked her again. Queen Victoria died in 1901.

Answer these questions:

Section A
1. When did Victoria become Queen?
2. Where was Victoria crowned?
3. Who did Queen Victoria marry?
4. How many children did she have?
5. When did Prince Albert die?
6. When had Victoria been Queen for 50 years?
7. When did Queen Victoria die?

Section B
1. Why do you think the Queen only wore black clothes after Albert died?
2. Why do you think the queen became disliked?

Section C
Carefully draw and colour a picture of Queen Victoria.

The Reign of Queen Victoria

Victoria became Queen on 20th June 1837, when she was 18 years old. The Archbishop of Canterbury hurried to Kensington Palace in the early morning to tell her that her uncle was dead and she was now the Queen of England. The people of Britain were delighted to have a young queen. Victoria was crowned on 28th June 1838. There was a ceremony held at Westminster Abbey.

Her cousin, Prince Albert, visited her in 1839 and they fell in love almost at once. They were married on 10th February 1840 in St. James' Palace. Between 1840 and 1857 she had nine children, four sons and five daughters. Albert was a very clever man and helped her to run the country.

In 1861 Prince Albert died. His death left the Queen very unhappy and for many years she only wore black clothes to show how she felt. She refused to live in London preferring to stay in her country houses. She also stopped appearing in public. This made the Queen very unpopular.

In 1887 Victoria completed 50 years as queen, and a great jubilee party was held for her. Wearing a black dress she was driven through the streets of London cheered by the people, now that she was seen in public again. Queen Victoria died on 22nd January 1901 having been on the English throne longer than any other king or queen.

Answer these questions:

Section A
1. When did Victoria become Queen?
2. Where was Victoria crowned?
3. Who did Queen Victoria marry?
4. How many children did she have?
5. When did Prince Albert die?
6. When had Victoria been queen for 50 years?
7. When did Queen Victoria die?
8. Where was Queen Victoria married?

Section B
1. Why do you think the Archbishop of Canterbury 'hurried' to Kensington Palace?
2. Why do you think the people of Britain were delighted to have a young queen?
3. Why do you think Victoria stopped appearing in public?
4. Why did this make her unpopular?

Section C
Carefully draw and colour a picture of Queen Victoria.

The Reign of Queen Victoria

Victoria became Queen on 20th June 1837, when she was 18 years old. The Archbishop of Canterbury and the Lord Chamberlain hurried to Kensington Palace in the early morning to tell her that William IV, her uncle, was dead and she was now the Queen of England. As she stood in her dressing gown and slippers, they knelt down, kissed her hand and saluted her as queen. The people of Britain were delighted to have a young queen after a succession of elderly and rather disreputable kings. Victoria was crowned on 28th June 1838. There was a great procession through London and a grand ceremony at Westminster Abbey.

At first she was very fond of quite frivolous pastimes. However, when her German cousin, Prince Albert, visited her in 1839 she fell in love with him almost at once. As it was not done for anyone to ask the queen to marry them, she proposed herself, something unheard of in those times! They were married on 10th February 1840 in the Chapel Royal at St. James's Palace. Between 1840 and 1857 she had nine children, four sons and five daughters. Albert was a very intelligent man and soon became a close adviser to the Queen.

Victoria was extremely fond of the highlands of Scotland and as the growing railways made travel much easier, she and Albert spent many holidays with their children at their house in Balmoral, in Aberdeenshire. They also built a house at Osborne on the Isle of Wight. The greatest grief in Victoria's life was in 1861 when Prince Albert died of typhoid fever. His death left the Queen deeply unhappy and for many years she only wore black clothes to show her grief. She refused to live in London preferring to shut herself away in her country houses. She also stopped going to public ceremonies. This made the Queen unpopular with her public.

In 1887 Victoria completed 50 years as queen, and a great jubilee was held for her. Wearing a black dress, she was driven through the streets of London cheered by her subjects now that she was seen in public again. Ten years later, another jubilee was held to celebrate 60 years of her reign. Queen Victoria died on 22nd January 1901 having reigned longer than any other English monarch.

In many ways Queen Victoria was a very stern woman, especially with her children. She is often remembered for the occassion when she described something she did not approve of by saying, "We are not amused!"

Answer these questions:

Section A
1. When did Victoria become Queen?
2. Where was Victoria crowned?
3. Who did Queen Victoria marry?
4. How many children did she have?
5. When did Prince Albert die?
6. When had Victoria been Queen for 50 years?
7. When did Queen Victoria die?
8. Where was Queen Victoria married?
9. Where did the Queen have her country houses?

Section B
1. Why do you think the Archbishop of Canterbury 'hurried' to Kensington Palace?
2. Why do you think the people of Britain were delighted to have a young queen?
3. Why do you think Victoria stopped appearing in public?
4. Why did this make her unpopular?
5. Why do you think Victoria was on the throne for so long?
6. What is a 'frivolous pastime'?
7. What is a 'disreputable king'?

Section C
Carefully draw and colour a picture of Queen Victoria.

Town and Country Life

In the country poor people lived in small cottages.

A man would work on a farm for 5p per day.

A woman would wash the clothes and cook the

meals. Many people moved to the towns to work

in the cotton mills. It was hard work and the pay

was poor. Lots of small houses were built for the

workers to live in. The dirty water made people ill

so a law was passed to provide clean drinking

water. During this time the towns grew much

bigger.

Copy this writing and fill in the gaps:

Town and Country Life

Poor people lived in small _____ in the country. A man would work for _____ per day on a farm. A woman would cook the meals and _____ the clothes. Many people moved to the _____ to work in the cotton mills. The pay was poor and the _____ hard. Lots of small houses were built for the _____ to live in. The dirty water made people ill so a law was passed to provide _____ drinking water. The towns grew much _____ during this time.

Town and Country Life

In the country some people lived in large houses with servants to do their jobs. The peasants lived in simple cottages grouped together in small villages.

A peasant might find work on a farm for as little as 5p per day. Women would clean the cottage, wash and mend the clothes, cook the meals and teach the children. The women also spun wool and wove cloth.

Families were often large and wages were low. Because life in the country was so difficult, many village people moved to the towns. Wool and cotton mills needed workers so many poor country people went to work in the mills. The conditions were hard and the pay was poor.

Rows of small terraced houses were built for the workers to live in. The water supply was often filthy and diseases spread easily. In 1875 a new law was passed to provide clean drinking water. This was a period of huge growth in the size of towns and cities.

Answer these questions:

Section A
1. Where did the peasants live?
2. How much would a peasant be paid each day?
3. What jobs did the women do?
4. Where did many country village people move to?
5. Where did the country people work in the towns?
6. Where did the country people live in the towns?
7. What made people in the towns become ill?

Section B
1. Why do you think many country people moved to the towns?
2. Why do you think a new law was passed in 1875?

Section C
Carefully draw and colour a picture of a country cottage.

Town and Country Life

In the country some people lived in large houses with servants to tend to their needs. Large farms would employ peasant villagers to help work the land. The peasants lived in simple cottages grouped together in small villages.

A peasant might find work on a farm for as little as 5p per day. Cottage gardens were used to grow vegetables and keep hens. Women would clean the house, wash and mend the clothes, cook the meals and teach the children. The women also spun wool and wove cloth.

Families were often large and wages were low resulting in great poverty. Because life in the country was so difficult, many village people flocked to the towns looking for a better way of life. In the towns, factories were making lots of new things. Wool and cotton mills were replacing the spinning and weaving previously done in village homes, so many poor people went to work in the mills. The conditions were hard and the pay was poor.

Rows of small terraced houses were built for the workers to live in. The water supply was often filthy and diseases such as cholera spread easily from house to house. In 1875 a new law was passed to improve the sewers and provide clean drinking water. This was a period of huge growth in the size of towns and cities.

Answer these questions:

Section A
1 Where did the peasants live?
2 How much would a peasant be paid each day?
3 What jobs did the women do?
4 Where did many country village people move to?
5 Where did the country people work in the towns?
6 Where did the country people live in the towns?
7 What made people in the towns become ill?
8 What did a new law change in 1875?

Section B
1 What do you think caused great poverty amongst the country village people?
2 What does the phrase 'flocked to the towns' mean?
3 What changes were happening in the towns to attract country people to move house?
4 Why do you think cholera was able to spread easily from house to house?

Section C
Carefully draw and colour a picture of a country cottage.

Town and Country Life

There was often great division of wealth between the people that lived in the country during Victorian Times. Some people owned large estates of land and lived in country houses with servants to tend to their needs. Large farms were created and farmed by the owner who would employ peasant villagers to help him to work the land. The peasants lived in simple cottages grouped together in small villages.

A peasant might find work on a farm as a labourer for as little as 5p per day. Even in those times this was not enough to feed a family, so his wife would work in the fields as well. Cottage gardens were used to supplement the food supply by growing vegetables and keeping hens. Some men worked as blacksmiths, tanners or carpenters. Women would clean the house, wash and mend the clothes, cook the meals and teach the children. The women also spun wool and wove cloth.

Families were often large and wages were low resulting in great poverty. Some families managed to get a child or two 'in service', which meant they were employed as a 'live in' servant in a large wealthy household. They would never be short of food but the working hours were long and they were rarely allowed home to visit their families. Because life in the country was so difficult, many village people flocked to the towns looking for a better way of life.

In the towns, factories powered by steam engines were manufacturing all manner of things. Wool and cotton mills were replacing the spinning and weaving previously done in village homes, so many poor people went to work there instead. There was often no work for the men because women and children could be employed for much lower wages. The conditions were hard and the pay was poor.

With new factories springing up everywhere, rows and rows of small terraced houses were built nearby for the workers to live in. The wealthy factory owners often lived further away in much larger mansions with their families and servants. At first the terraced houses suffered from poor sanitation. The water supply was often filthy and diseases such as cholera spread easily from house to house. In 1875 a new law was passed by the Government to force each town to clean up the drains and sewers. New water pipes were installed to make sure the drinking water was clean. This was a period of huge growth in the size of towns and cities.

Answer these questions:

Section A
1. Where did the peasants live?
2. How much would a peasant be paid each day?
3. What jobs did the women do?
4. Where did many country village people move to?
5. Where did the country people work in the towns?
6. Where did the country people live in the towns?
7. What made people in the towns become ill?
8. What did a new law change in 1875?
9. Why was there often no work for the men in the factories and mills?

Section B
1. What do you think caused great poverty amongst the country village people?
2. What does the phrase 'flocked to the towns' mean?
3. What changes were happening in the towns to attract country people to move house?
4. Why do you think cholera was able to spread so easily from house to house?
5. How do you think a peasant would feel about working for a wealthy farmer?
6. Define the words 'blacksmith', 'tanner' and 'carpenter'.
7. Why do you think factory owners did not live close to the factories?

Section C
Carefully draw and colour a picture of a country cottage.

Everyday Life in a Terraced Row

These houses had the toilet outside. The girls would share one bed and the boys another. Coal fires would heat the house. Monday was washday. Hot water and flat irons were heated on the fire. These houses did not have a bathroom.

A tin tub would be placed in front of the fire and filled with hot water. The girls would be sent to bed early and the boys would take turns to have a bath. Homes had oil or gas lights. Even poor homes had curtains and rugs.

Copy this writing and fill in the gaps:

Everyday Life in a Terraced Row

The _____ was outside the house. The boys would share one _____ and the girls another. The house was heated with coal _____. Washday was _____. Flat irons and hot _____ were heated on the fire. These houses did not have a _____. A tin _____ filled with hot water would be placed in front of the fire. The boys would take turns to have a _____ after the girls had been sent to bed early. Homes had _____ or oil lights. Even poor homes had _____ and curtains.

Everyday Life in a Terraced Row

Victorian terraced houses had an outside toilet and no garden. All water came from an outside pump. The houses were small but families were large. The girls would share one bed and the boys another. Coal fires would heat the house.

Monday was washday. Hot water was heated on the fire to fill a tub. The clothes were moved around in the hot water using a 'dolly peg' and dried inside on a clothes rack. Flat irons were heated on the fire.

Terraced houses did not have a bathroom. A tin tub would be placed in front of the fire and filled with hot water. The girls would be sent to bed early and the boys would take turns to use the same water to bathe in. On another evening the boys would go to bed early and the girls would bathe.

Victorian homes had no electricity with light being provided by oil or gas lights. Even poor homes had curtains and rugs, which at the time were seen as luxuries.

Answer these questions:

Section A
1. Where was the toilet in a Victorian terraced house?
2. Where did the drinking water come from?
3. Where did the girls sleep?
4. Where did hot water to wash their clothes come from?
5. What did they use for a bath?
6. Why were the girls sometimes sent to bed early?
7. How were Victorian terraced houses lit?

Section B
1. How do you think children would feel about going to the toilet in the winter?
2. How do you think children would feel about having a bath in the living room in front of the fire?

Section C
Carefully draw and colour a picture of a terraced row.

Everyday Life in a Terraced Row

The poorer houses in the towns were usually small terraced houses with no gardens and an outside closet (toilet). Water was collected from an outside pump. The houses were not large having one or two rooms downstairs with the same above. Families however were large, often with six or seven children, so few had a bed of their own. The girls would share one bed and the boys another. Coal fires would heat the house.

Washday would normally be on a Monday when hot water was heated on the fire to fill a tub. The clothes were moved around in the hot water using a 'dolly peg' and dried inside on a clothes rack. Flat irons were heated on the fire. The oven, also heated by the fire, was used to make bread.

Terraced houses did not have a bathroom. A tin tub would be placed in front of the fire and filled with hot water. The girls would be sent to bed early and the boys would take turns to use the same water to bathe in. On another evening the boys would go to bed early and the girls would bathe.

Victorian homes had no electricity with light being provided by oil or gas lights. The growth of factories, which made goods cheaply, meant that even poor homes could now afford some luxuries such as curtains and rugs.

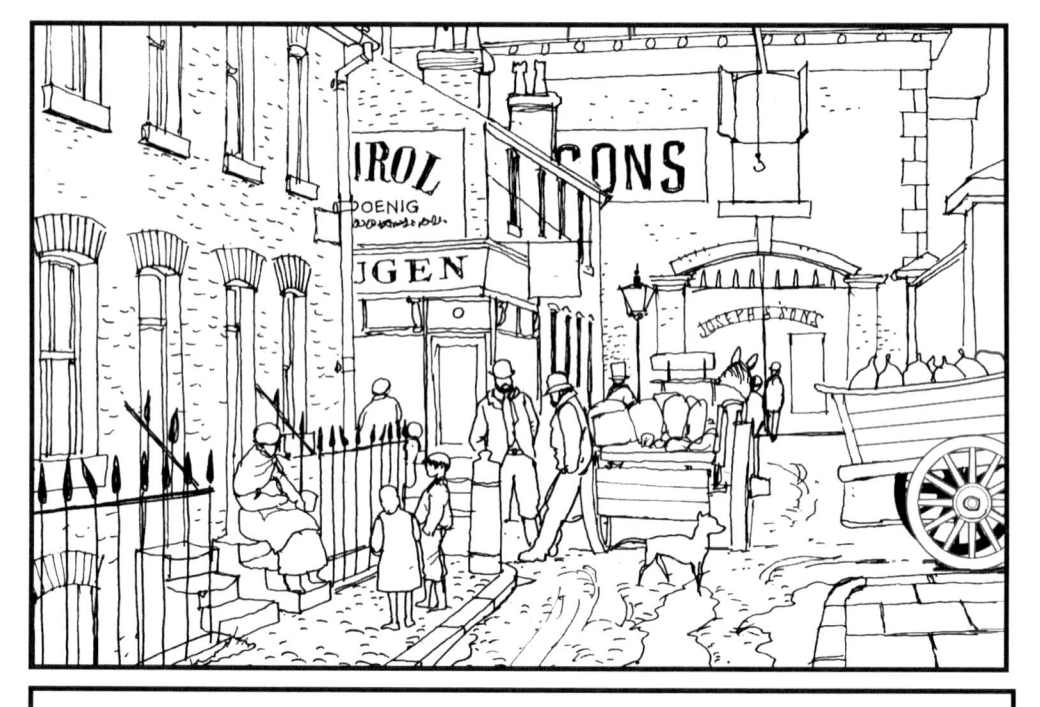

Answer these questions:

Section A
1 Where was the toilet in a Victorian terraced house?
2 Where did the drinking water come from?
3 Where did the girls sleep?
4 Where did hot water to wash their clothes come from?
5 What did they use for a bath?
6 Why were the girls sometimes sent to bed early?
7 How were Victorian terraced houses lit?
8 What luxuries did even poor homes have?

Section B
1 How do you think children would feel about going to the toilet in the winter?
2 How do you think children would feel about having a bath in the living room in front of the fire?
3 What do you think the inside of the house would be like on washday?
4 How did factories make luxuries possible for poor people?

Section C
Carefully draw and colour a picture of a terraced row.

Everyday Life in a Terraced Row

The poorer houses in the towns were usually small terraced houses with no gardens and an outside closet (toilet). This may even have been shared. Water supplies were also shared with many families using the same outside pump. In this way diseases were easily spread.

The houses were not large having one or two rooms downstairs with the same above. Families however were large, six or seven children being the norm, so few had the luxury of a bed of their own. The girls would share one bed and the boys another. Sometimes an additional 'bed-place' could be found in the cupboard under the stairs.

The house would be heated by coal fires, which also provided heat for cooking and hot water.

Large families required lots of cooking and washing, all of which was hard work. Washday would typically be on a Monday when large quantities of hot water were heated on the fire to fill a tub. The clothes were moved around in the hot water using a 'dolly peg'. Next they were rinsed and dried inside, hung on a clothes rack. Flat irons, again heated on the coal fire, would be used to iron the clothes when dry. A metal hob could be swung over the fire to heat a kettle or a pan. The oven, also heated by the fire, was used to make bread.

Terraced houses did not have the luxury of a bathroom. A tin tub would be placed in front of the fire and filled with hot water. The girls would be sent to bed early and the boys would take turns to use the same water to bathe in. On another evening the boys would go to bed early and the girls would bathe.

Victorian homes had no electricity with light being provided by oil or gaslights. The growth of factories which mass produced goods meant that even humble homes could now afford some luxuries such as curtains and rugs. However, because most homes were rented, many lived in fear of getting behind with the rent and eventually being put out on the street.

Answer these questions:

Section A
1. Where was the toilet in a Victorian terraced house?
2. Where did the drinking water come from?
3. Where did the girls sleep?
4. Where did hot water to wash their clothes come from?
5. What did they use for a bath?
6. Why were the girls sometimes sent to bed early?
7. How were Victorian terraced houses lit?
8. What luxuries did even poor homes have?
9. What did many people live in fear of?

Section B
1. How do you think children would feel about going to the toilet in the winter?
2. How do you think children would feel about having a bath in the living room in front of the fire?
3. What do you think the inside of the house would be like on washday?
4. How did factories make luxuries possible for poor people?
5. What are the disadvantages of many people living in a very small house?
6. Define the terms 'dolly-peg' and 'flat-iron'.
7. Why would a wealthy Victorian not choose to live in a terraced row?

Section C
Carefully draw and colour a picture of a terraced row.

Everyday Life in a Wealthy Home

Some wealthy families lived in large terraced

houses with a servant to do the housework.

Wealthy children did not go to school, they were

taught at home. The servant lit fires, polished

shoes, swept floors, scrubbed steps, polished

cutlery and filled baths with hot water. Some

children would spend most of their time in the

nursery looked after by a nanny. They would have

toys such as jigsaws, a toy theatre, clockwork

models and a rocking horse to play with.

Copy this writing and fill in the gaps:

Everyday Life in a Wealthy Home

In large terraced houses, some wealthy families had a servant to do the _____. Wealthy children were taught at _____ and did not go to _____. The servant lit fires, swept _____, polished shoes, scrubbed _____, polished cutlery, and filled baths with _____ water. The nanny looked after the children most of the time in the _____. They would have toys such as a _____ horse, a toy theatre, _____ models and jigsaws to play with.

Everyday Life in a Wealthy Home

Some wealthy families lived in larger terraced houses and enjoyed gardens, their own water taps and gas lighting. These homes would have a 'maid of all work' to do the housework.

Wealthy children would not go to school. Instead a governess would be employed to teach them at home. As they got older the boys would be sent away to boarding school whilst the girls stayed at home to learn needlework, piano playing and how to run a home.

The servants started working very early so they could light the coal fires ready for the family getting up. Other jobs included polishing shoes, sweeping floors, scrubbing steps, polishing cutlery and filling baths with hot water.

Some children would spend most of their time in the nursery looked after by a nanny. They would have toys such as jigsaws, a toy theatre, clockwork models and a rocking horse to play with.

Answer these questions:

Section A
1. Where did some wealthy families live?
2. What did the 'maid of all work' do?
3. What did the governess do?
4. What did the girls learn as they got older?
5. Why did the servants start work very early?
6. Name some of the jobs done by a servant.
7. What sort of toys would be found in the nursery?

Section B
1. How do you think a servant would feel about starting early to heat the house before the family got up?
2. Would you prefer to be taught at home or at school? Give reasons for your answer.

Section C
Carefully draw and colour a picture of some nursery toys.

Everyday Life in a Wealthy Home

Not all families were poor in Victorian times. Some families lived in larger terraced houses with gardens back and front and enjoyed such luxuries as their own water taps and gas lighting. These homes would have a 'maid of all work' who slept in the attic and whose job was to do the housework.

Wealthy children would not go to school. Instead a tutor or governess would be employed to teach them at home. As they got older the boys would be sent away to boarding school whilst the girls stayed at home to learn needlework, piano playing and how to run a home.

The servants started working very early so they could make the coal fires ready for the family getting up. Other jobs included polishing shoes, sweeping floors, scrubbing steps and polishing cutlery. If a member of the family wanted a bath the water had to be heated over a fire and carried upstairs in jugs until the bath was full.

Some children would spend most of their time in the nursery looked after by a nanny. They would have toys such as jigsaws, a toy theatre, clockwork models and a rocking horse to play with. Their meals would be served to them here and not until they began their schooling would they have meals with their parents.

Answer these questions:

Section A
1. Where did some wealthy families live?
2. What did the 'maid of all work' do?
3. What did the governess do?
4. What did the girls learn as they got older?
5. Why did the servants start work very early?
6. Name some of the jobs done by a servant.
7. What sort of toys would be found in the nursery?
8. Where did the children eat their meals?

Section B
1. How do you think a servant would feel about starting early to light the fires and heat the house before the family got up?
2. Would you prefer to be taught at home or at school? Give reasons for your answer.
3. Why do you think 'water taps' and 'gas lights' are described as luxuries?
4. What do you think it would be like to be sent to boarding school?

Section C
Carefully draw and colour a picture of some nursery toys.

Level 4   © Topical Resources. May be photocopied for classroom use only

Everyday Life in a Wealthy Home

Not all families were poor in Victorian times. Some families lived in larger terraced houses with small gardens back and front and enjoyed such luxuries as their own water taps and gas lighting. These homes would have a 'maid of all work' who slept in the attic and whose job was to do the housework.

The wealthiest families built large mansion type houses in the more pleasant parts of the town. These houses would have attics and basements for various servants to live and work in with a second set of stairs at the back of the house for the servants to use. The children that lived in these homes were well protected from the terrible poverty found in the streets nearby.

Wealthy children would not go to school. Instead a tutor or governess would be employed to teach them at home. As they got older the boys would be sent away to boarding school whilst the girls stayed at home to learn needlework, piano playing and how to run a home. The team of servants, each with different jobs to do, would attend the family. Teenage country girls would take jobs as maids to 'see the world', send a little money home to help feed large families and hopefully find a husband.

For the servants the working day started very early so they could clean the grates and make the coal fires ready for the family getting up. The days were long being filled with manual tasks including polishing shoes, sweeping floors, scrubbing steps and polishing cutlery. If a member of the family wanted a bath the water had to be heated over a fire and carried upstairs in jugs until the bath was full.

Some children would spend most of their time in the nursery looked after by a nanny. They would have toys such as jigsaws, a toy theatre, clockwork models and a rocking horse to play with. Their meals would be served to them here and not until they were of tutoring age would they have meals with their parents.

Many large houses in Victorian times were built in various different styles often with turrets, balconies and iron railings added for effect. The inside decoration was very fussy containing many ornate pictures and items of furniture. The more wealthy homes were beginning to include luxuries such as bathrooms, lavatories and hot water systems.

Answer these questions:

Section A
1. Where did some wealthy families live?
2. What did the 'maid of all work' do?
3. What did the governess do?
4. What did the girls learn as they got older?
5. Why did the servants start work very early?
6. Name some of the jobs done by a servant.
7. What sort of toys would be found in the nursery?
8. Where did the children eat their meals?
9. What was added to decorate the outside of some wealthy Victorian homes?

Section B
1. How do you think a servant would feel about starting early to light the fires and heat the house before the family got up?
2. Would you prefer to be taught at home or at school? Give reasons for your answer.
3. Why do you think 'water taps' and 'gas lights' are described as luxuries?
4. What do you think it would be like to be sent to boarding school?
5. Why do you think servants were asked to use different stairs from the family?
6. Define the terms 'tutor' and 'governess'.
7. Why do you think country girls were 'seeing the world' when they took a job as a servant in a wealthy home?

Section C
Carefully draw and colour a picture of some nursery toys.

Children at Work

Many women and children had to work because they were poor. Women and children were used to move the heavy carts in the coal mines.

Children collected loose cotton in mills. Small boys were sent up chimneys to clean them out.

Other jobs included sweeping the street, holding waiting horses, shining shoes, begging or even stealing. Lord Shaftesbury tried to improve things. In 1842 a law was passed to stop children under 10 working in mines. Slowly, things began to get better for working children.

Copy this writing and fill in the gaps:

Children at Work

Because they were poor, many women and _____ had to work. Women and children were used to move the heavy carts in the _____ mines. In the mills, children collected loose _____. Small boys were sent up _____ to clean them out. Other jobs included holding waiting horses, sweeping the _____, begging, shining shoes or even stealing. Lord _____ tried to improve things. A law was passed to stop _____ under 10 working in mines in 1842. Slowly, things began to get better for _____ children.

Level 2

© Topical Resources. May be photocopied for classroom use only.

page 18

Children at Work

Poverty and hunger meant that many women and children had to work to help the family survive.

Women and children were used to move the heavy carts of coal in the coal mines. Children who worked in mills had to crawl around under noisy machinery collecting loose cotton. Small boys were sent up chimneys to clean them out.

The days were long for working children often lasting twelve or fourteen hours. Many poor children could be seen on the streets sweeping the road clean for any lady or gentlemen wishing to cross. Other jobs included holding waiting horses, shining shoes, begging or even stealing.

Lord Shaftesbury tried to improve the lot of working children. In 1833 a law was passed banning children under 9 working in mills. In 1840 a law was passed forbidding children to be used to clean chimneys. In 1842 a law was passed to stop children under 10 working in mines.

Answer these questions:

Section A
1. Why did many women and children have to work?
2. What did children do in the coal mines?
3. What did children have to do in cotton mills?
4. Why were small boys sent up chimneys?
5. How long would children work in a day?
6. Who tried to improve things for working children?
7. What happened in 1833?

Section B
1. What do you think it would be like for a small child working in a coal mine?
2. Why do you think Lord Shaftesbury tried to change things?

Section C
Carefully draw and colour a picture of a child at work.

Children at Work

Poverty and hunger, caused by having large families and poorly paid work for the men, meant that many women and children had to work to help the family survive.

Children could start work as young as six or seven years old. Women and children were used to move the heavy carts of coal in the coal mines. Children who worked in mills had to crawl around under noisy machinery collecting loose cotton. One wrong move could result in an arm or your hair being caught in the moving machinery! Small boys were sent up chimneys to clean them out.

The working days were long for children often lasting twelve or fourteen hours a day. Many poor children could be seen on the streets of the big towns and cities sweeping the road clean for any lady or gentlemen wishing to cross, holding bridles for waiting horses, shining shoes, begging or even stealing.

Lord Shaftesbury tried to improve the lot of working children. In 1833 a law was passed banning children under the age of 9 working in mills. In 1840 a law was passed forbidding children to be used to clean chimneys. In 1842 a law was passed to stop children under the age of 10 working in mines. It was eventually agreed that children under the age of thirteen must not work longer than eight hours a day.

Answer these questions:

Section A
1 Why did many women and children have to work?
2 What did children do in the coal mines?
3 What did children have to do in cotton mills?
4 Why were small boys sent up chimneys?
5 How long would children work in a day?
6 Who tried to improve things for working children?
7 What happened in 1833?
8 When were children forbidden to clean chimneys?

Section B
1 What do you think it would be like for a small child working in a coal mine?
2 Why do you think Lord Shaftesbury tried to change things?
3 What made working in a mill so dangerous?
4 What sort of jobs did children do on the street?

Section C
Carefully draw and colour a picture of a child at work.

Level 4   © **Topical Resources.** May be photocopied for classroom use only.   page 20

Children at Work

In the first half of Queen Victoria's long reign there were a great many poor people in the big factory towns. Poverty and hunger, caused by having large families and poorly paid work for the men, meant that many women and children had to work to help the family survive.

Children could start work as young as six or seven years old. Women and children were used to move the heavy carts of coal in the coal mines. It was dirty, heavy work which required a lot of bending down. Small boys would sit for hours on their own in cold, wet and draughty tunnels operating trap doors to provide ventilation for the mines. Children who worked in mills had to crawl around under noisy machinery collecting loose cotton. This work was extremely dangerous as one wrong move could result in a limb or your hair being caught in the moving machinery!

Small boys were sent up chimneys to clean them out. To prepare them for this their master would rub salt water into their knees and elbows until they bled. Repeatedly doing this made the skin grow hard but it was an extremely painful process.

The working days were long for children often lasting twelve or fourteen hours. Many poor children could be seen on the streets of the big towns and cities sweeping the road clean for any lady or gentlemen wishing to cross, holding bridles for waiting horses, shining shoes, begging or even stealing.

During Victoria's long reign many people tried to improve the lot of working children. Lord Shaftesbury was one of these. In 1833 a law was passed banning children under 9 years working in mills. In 1840 a law was passed forbidding children to be used to clean chimneys, but these laws were hard to enforce and ignored by many people. In 1842 a law was passed to stop children under 10 years working in mines. As more and more social reformers became aware of the plight of working children conditions improved, and it was eventually agreed that children under the age of thirteen must not work longer than eight hours a day.

It was some time before much notice was taken of the new laws, but gradually throughout Queen Victoria's reign working conditions improved, especially for poor children.

Answer these questions:

Section A
1. Why did many women and children have to work?
2. What did children do in the coal mines?
3. What did children have to do in cotton mills?
4. Why were small boys sent up chimneys?
5. How long would children work in a day?
6. Who tried to improve things for working children?
7. What happened in 1833?
8. When were children forbidden to clean chimneys?
9. What happened in 1842?

Section B
1. What do you think it would be like for a small child working in a coal mine?
2. Why do you think Lord Shaftesbury tried to change things?
3. What made working in a mill so dangerous?
4. What sort of jobs did children do on the street?
5. Why was it cruel to use small boys to clean chimneys?
6. Why do you think the new laws were hard to enforce?
7. How long did it take for things to improve for working children?

Section C
Carefully draw and colour a picture of a child at work.

School for All

In 1870 a law was passed which said that all children must go to school. Parents were expected to pay a penny a day but this was hard for poor families. Some children worked half the day and went to school for the other half. The children sat in rows. A teacher may have 70 pupils in a class. School was very strict with children getting the cane for doing wrong things. Children were taught to read, do sums and learn the Bible.

Copy this writing and fill in the gaps:

School for All

All children had to go to school after a law was passed in _____. It was hard for poor families as they were expected to pay a _____ a day. Some children went to school for half the day and went to _____ for the other half. The children sat in _____. A teacher may have _____ pupils in a class. School was very strict with children getting the _____ for doing wrong things. Children were taught to read, do _____ and learn the Bible.

School for All

Some schools were built before Victorian times but they were only for the rich. In 1870 a law was passed which said that all children between five and thirteen must go to school.

School boards were set up to build new schools. Parents were expected to pay a penny a day but this did not go down well with those who were poor. Some children, called half-timers, worked half the day and went to school for the other half.

Victorian schools were different from today's schools. The children sat in rows or stood in groups to be taught. A teacher may be in charge of between 60 to 80 pupils with monitors (older children) paid to help.

The teacher would keep control from a raised up desk from where he or she could see the whole class. School was very strict with children getting the cane for doing anything wrong. Children were taught to read, do sums and learn the Bible.

Answer these questions:

Section A
1 Did schools exist before Victorian times?
2 What happened in 1870?
3 How much were parents expected to pay for school?
4 What was a 'half-timer'?
5 How many children may be in one class?
6 Why was the teacher's desk raised up?
7 What were children taught in school?

Section B
1 Why do you think some parents were not happy to send their children to school?
2 Would you like to attend a Victorian School? Give reasons for your answer.

Section C
Carefully draw and colour a picture of children at school.

School for All

Schools had existed for many years before Victorian times but they were only for the wealthy. Churches started 'Sunday Schools' to teach children who worked through the week. In 1870 a law was passed which said that all children between the ages of five and thirteen must go to school.

School boards were set up to build schools in areas where there were none. Parents were expected to pay a penny a day but this did not go down well with those who were poor. Some children, called half-timers, worked half the day and attended school for the other half.

Victorian schools were different from today's schools. The children sat in rows or stood in groups to be taught. A teacher may be in charge of between 60 to 80 pupils with monitors (older children) paid to help. The teacher would keep control from a raised up desk from where he or she could see the whole class. Discipline was very strict with children receiving a beating from the teacher using a cane for even minor offences.

Once a year the school inspector would come to test the children to see if they had reached the 'Standard' to move into the next class. If not, they would repeat the year resulting in children of various ages being mixed together. Children were taught to read, do sums and learn scripture.

Answer these questions:

Section A
1. Did schools exist before Victorian times?
2. What happened in 1870?
3. How much were parents expected to pay for school?
4. What was a 'half-timer'?
5. How many children may be in one class?
6. Why was the teacher's desk raised up?
7. What were children taught in school?
8. Why did the school inspector visit once a year?

Section B
1. Why do you think some parents were not happy to send their children to school?
2. Would you like to attend a Victorian School? Give reasons for your answer.
3. How would you feel about school on Sunday if you were at work during the week?
4. How would you feel about an Inspector making you repeat a year?

Section C
Carefully draw and colour a picture of children at school.

Level 4   © Topical Resources. May be photocopied for classroom use only.

School for All

Schools had existed for many years before Victorian times but they were only for the wealthy. Public schools existed for those that could afford the high fees. Merchants and other high earners would pay to send boys to the Grammar School. Other children were taught at home by tutors or governesses.

Girls' schools were few in number. They taught deportment (how to walk and sit gracefully), manners, needlework, dancing and a little music and reading. For the most part, girls were expected to learn at home how to run a house, how to cook and how to make jams, wines and simple medicines.

Some villages had Dame Schools where an older lady would teach a number of small children in one room of her house. Some factory owners provided schools for the children of their workers. Churches started Sunday Schools to teach children who worked through the week to read the Bible. Out of these grew the church day schools but many children still received no schooling at all.

In 1870 a law was passed which said that all children between the ages of five and thirteen must go to school. School boards were set up to build schools in areas where there were none. Parents were expected to pay a penny or two a day but this did not go down well with those who needed the income from their children being out at work. Some children, called half-timers, worked half the day and attended school for the other half.

Victorian schools were different from today's schools. The children sat in rows or stood in groups to be taught. A teacher may be in charge of between 60 to 80 pupils with monitors (older children) paid to help. Classes of up to 100 pupils were not unheard of! The teacher would keep control from a raised up desk from where he or she could see the whole class. Discipline was very strict with children receiving a beating from the teacher using a cane for even minor offences.

The children did not work in age groups but in Standards. Once a year the school inspector would come to test the children to see if they had reached 'Standard' to move into the next class. If not, they would repeat the year resulting in children of various ages being mixed together. Children were taught to read, do sums, mental arithmetic and scripture.

Answer these questions:

Section A
1. Did schools exist before Victorian times?
2. What happened in 1870?
3. How much were parents expected to pay for school?
4. What was a 'half-timer'?
5. How many children may be in one class?
6. Why was the teacher's desk raised up?
7. What were children taught in school?
8. Why did the school inspector visit once a year?
9. What did girls' schools teach?

Section B
1. Why do you think some parents were not happy to send their children to school?
2. Would you like to attend a Victorian School? Give reasons for your answer.
3. How would you feel about school on Sunday if you were at work during the week?
4. How would you feel about an Inspector making you repeat a year?
5. Why do you think girls' schools were few in number?
6. Why do you think factory owners provided schools for the children of workers?
7. What is a 'merchant'?

Section C
Carefully draw and colour a picture of children at school.

The Workhouse

In Victorian times people who had no work were sent to the workhouse. These were large buildings where the poorest people lived. Food in the workhouse was free but you had to give up living with your own family. You also had to give up your own clothes and wear a workhouse uniform. Husbands, wives, parents and children were split up. They were made to do hard work such as breaking up stones to build new roads. The food was very poor and there was only just enough of it to stay alive.

Copy this writing and fill in the gaps:

The Workhouse

People who had no work in Victorian times were sent to the _____. These were large buildings where the poorest people _____. In the workhouse you had to give up living with your own _____ but the food was free. You also had to wear a workhouse _____ and give up your own clothes. Wives, _____, parents and children were split up. They were made to do hard work such as breaking up _____ to build new roads. The food was very poor and there was only just enough of it to stay _____.

The Workhouse

In Victorian times people who had no work were sent to the workhouse. These were grim buildings where the poorest people lived.

Food in the workhouse was free but you had to give up living with your own family. You also had to give up your own clothes and wear a workhouse uniform. Men wore striped cotton shirts, jackets, trousers and a cloth cap. Women wore blue and white striped dresses underneath a smock. Shoes were provided.

Husbands, wives, parents and children were split up. They slept in dormitories and were made to do hard work such as breaking up stones to build new roads. The food was very poor and there was barely enough of it to stay alive.

Visitors to the workhouse urged the government to improve conditions. One improvement meant that children were allowed to attend school but their untidy appearance made them stand out.

Answer these questions:

Section A
1. Where were people sent if they had no work?
2. What did you give up to live in a workhouse?
3. What did people wear in the workhouse?
4. Where did people sleep in the workhouse?
5. What sort of work was done in the workhouse?
6. What was the food like in the workhouse?
7. What improvements were made to the workhouse?

Section B
1. How do you think people would have felt if they were sent to live in a workhouse?
2. What do you think would be the worst thing about living in a workhouse?

Section C
Carefully draw and colour a picture of a workhouse.

The Workhouse

In Victorian times people who had no work received no money at all. If they were old, sick, orphaned or simply could not find any work they were sent to the workhouse. These were grim buildings where the poorest people lived.

Food and accommodation in the workhouse was free but you had to give up living with your own family. You also had to give up your own clothes and wear a workhouse uniform. Men wore striped cotton shirts, jackets, trousers and a cloth cap. Women wore blue and white striped dresses underneath a smock. Shoes were provided.

Husbands, wives, parents and children were split up. They slept in dormitories and were made to do long tedious work such as crushing animal bones to make fertilizer or breaking up stones to build new roads. The food was very poor and there was barely enough of it to stay alive.

Discipline was strict. For swearing, or pretending to be ill, your food would be reduced for up to two days. For more serious offences, such as fighting, you could be beaten with a wooden rod! Visitors to the workhouse urged the government to improve conditions. One improvement meant that children were allowed to attend the local Board School but their untidy appearance made them stand out.

Answer these questions:

Section A
1　Where were people sent if they had no work?
2　What did you give up to live in a workhouse?
3　What did people wear in the workhouse?
4　Where did people sleep in the workhouse?
5　What sort of work was done in the workhouse?
6　What was the food like in the workhouse?
7　What improvements were made to the workhouse?
8　How were people punished in the workhouse?

Section B
1　How do you think people would have felt if they were sent to live in a workhouse?
2　What do you think would be the worst thing about living in a workhouse?
3　How would a workhouse child feel in the Board School?
4　What is fertilizer?

Section C
Carefully draw and colour a picture of a workhouse.

The Workhouse

In Victorian times people who had no work received no money at all. If they were old, sick, orphaned or simply could not find any work they were sent to the workhouse. These were grim buildings where the destitute lived and worked. People feared being sent to the workhouse. The government of the time believed that people without work should not be fed or housed any better than the poorest wage earner. The problem was, some wages were very low indeed!

Food and accommodation in the workhouse was free but you had to give up responsibility for your own family. The residents also had to give up their own clothes and wear a workhouse uniform. Men wore striped cotton shirts, jackets, trousers and a cloth cap. Women wore blue and white striped dresses underneath a smock. Shoes were provided.

Husbands, wives, parents and children were split up. They slept in dormitories and were made to do long, tedious work such as crushing animal bones to make fertilizer or breaking up stones to build new roads. Children were sometimes apprenticed to local factories where they slept in shifts. This means one set of children were in bed while another set were working. The food was very poor and there was barely enough of it to stay alive.

Discipline was strict. For swearing or pretending to be ill your food would be reduced for up to two days. For more serious offences, such as fighting, you could be beaten with a wooden rod! Visitors to the workhouse urged the government to improve conditions. Some improvements were made. Old married couples who had spent most of their lives together were to be given a room to share, but this was often not the case. Girls and boys were allowed to attend the local Board School but they stood out from the other children with their cropped hair and untidy appearance.

In many ways the treatment in a workhouse was little different from that in a prison, leaving many inmates feeling that they were being punished for the crime of poverty. However, during the course of Victoria's reign, conditions slowly improved but it wasn't until the 20th Century that the workhouse was finally abolished and replaced by the new Social Security system.

Answer these questions:

Section A
1. Where were people sent if they had no work?
2. What did you give up to live in a workhouse?
3. What did people wear in the workhouse?
4. Where did people sleep in the workhouse?
5. What sort of work was done in the workhouse?
6. What was the food like in the workhouse?
7. What improvements were made to the workhouse?
8. How were people punished in the workhouse?
9. When was the workhouse finally abolished?

Section B
1. How do you think people would have felt if they were sent to live in a workhouse?
2. What do you think would be the worst thing about living in a workhouse?
3. How would a workhouse child feel in the Board School?
4. What is fertilizer?
5. Why do you think people feared being sent to the workhouse?
6. What is 'tedious work'?
7. What does the phrase 'apprenticed to local factories' mean?

Section C
Carefully draw and colour a picture of a workhouse.

New Inventions and the Great Exhibition

In Victorian times many new inventions came along. Rowland Hill invented the Penny Post. In 1876, the telephone was invented by Alexander Graham Bell. Other inventions included gramophones, moving pictures, sewing machines, typewriters and the fountain pen. In 1851 Queen Victoria opened an exhibition in the 'Crystal Palace'. It had over eight miles of display tables. On display were all sorts of new inventions including false teeth. The exhibition was very popular and over six million people came to visit.

Copy this writing and fill in the gaps:

New Inventions and the Great Exhibition

Many new _____ came along in Victorian times. The Penny Post was invented by _____ Hill. The telephone was invented by Alexander _____ Bell in 1876. Other inventions included typewriters, _____, gramophones, sewing machines and the _____ pen. Queen Victoria opened an exhibition in the 'Crystal _____' in 1851. It had over eight miles of _____ tables. On display were all sorts of new inventions including false _____. The exhibition was very popular and over _____ million people came to visit.

© Topical Resources. May be photocopied for classroom use only.

New Inventions and the Great Exhibition

In Victorian times many new inventions came along. Rowland Hill invented the Penny Post. The letter was paid for when posted and this led to the use of the first postage stamps and envelopes.

In 1876, the telephone was invented by Alexander Graham Bell. Other inventions included gramophones, moving pictures, sewing machines, typewriters and the fountain pen.

In 1851 Queen Victoria opened the first world trade exhibition in the 'Crystal Palace'. The exhibition was housed in a building that looked like a giant glass conservatory. It had over eight miles of display tables. On display were all manner of new inventions and manufactured goods including false teeth and artificial legs from America.

The exhibition was a great success and over six million people came to visit. At first just the more wealthy people came but these were soon followed by lots of ordinary working people travelling by train or even on foot.

Answer these questions:

Section A
1. What came along in Victorian times?
2. Who invented the Penny Post?
3. When was the telephone invented?
4. Name some other new inventions.
5. What happened in 1851?
6. What did the 'Crystal Palace' look like?
7. How many people visited the exhibition?

Section B
1. What do you think a postage stamp attached to an envelope proved?
2. Why do you think only wealthy people came to the exhibition at first?

Section C
Carefully draw and colour a picture of the 'Crystal Palace'.

New Inventions and the Great Exhibition

In Victorian times many new inventions came along. Rowland Hill invented the Penny Post. The letter was paid for when posted and this led to the use of the first postage stamps and envelopes.

A man called Wheatstone invented telegraphy, the method of passing a message along a wire. In 1876, the telephone was invented by Alexander Graham Bell. Other inventions included gramophones, moving pictures, sewing machines, typewriters and the fountain pen.

In 1851 Queen Victoria opened the first world trade exhibition in the 'Crystal Palace'. The idea for the exhibition came from Prince Albert, the Queen's husband. He wanted to show the world the new ideas and inventions being made. The exhibition was housed in a building that looked like a giant glass conservatory. It had over eight miles of display tables. On display were all manner of new inventions and manufactured goods including false teeth and artificial legs from America.

The exhibition was a great success. Over 19,000 different goods were displayed and over 6 million people came to visit. At first just the more wealthy people came but these were soon followed by lots of ordinary working people travelling by train or just on foot.

Answer these questions:

Section A
1 What came along in Victorian times?
2 Who invented the Penny Post?
3 When was the telephone invented?
4 Name some other new inventions.
5 What happened in 1851?
6 What did the 'Crystal Palace' look like?
7 How many people visited the exhibition?
8 What is telegraphy?

Section B
1 What do you think a postage stamp attached to an envelope proved?
2 Why do you think only wealthy people came to the exhibition at first?
3 What do you think people thought when they saw the first telephones?
4 Why did Prince Albert decide to hold a great exhibition?

Section C
Carefully draw and colour a picture of the 'Crystal Palace'.

New Inventions and the Great Exhibition

Before Victorian times most goods were made by hand by people working from their own homes. The steam engine changed all this. The railways improved the ability to trade and many new inventions came along.

Rowland Hill invented the Penny Post. A letter cost a penny no matter how far it had to travel. The letter was paid for when posted and this led to the use of the first postage stamps and envelopes. The first British stamp bore the head of the young Queen Victoria, and was called the Penny Black.

A man called Wheatstone invented telegraphy, the method of passing a message along a wire. The first telegraph service was installed in 1838. Later, in 1876, the telephone was invented by Alexander Graham Bell. Other inventions included gramophones, moving pictures, sewing machines, typewriters and the fountain pen. The first underground railway was built under the streets of London and opened in 1863.

In 1851 Queen Victoria opened the first world trade exhibition in the 'Crystal Palace' built on Hyde Park in London. It was called 'The Great Exhibition of the Works of Industry of All Nations'. The idea for the exhibition came from Prince Albert, the Queen's husband. He wanted to show the world the new ideas and inventions being built in Britain at this time and give the British people the opportunity to see what other countries had to offer.

The exhibition was housed in a building that looked like a giant glass conservatory. It was so tall that 30 metre elm trees grew inside it. It had over eight miles of display tables. On display were all manner of new inventions and manufactured goods including false teeth and artificial legs from America. Other exhibits included furniture, clothing, model cottages, clocks, silver, ribbons, lace, porcelain, embroideries etc. from many parts of the world.

The exhibition was a great success. Over 19,000 different goods were displayed and over 6 million people came to visit. At first just the more wealthy people came but these were soon followed by lots of ordinary working people travelling by train or just on foot. The event was considered such a success that soon other countries copied the idea.

Answer these questions:

Section A
1. What came along in Victorian times after the railways improved ability to trade?
2. Who invented the Penny Post?
3. When was the telephone invented?
4. Name some other new inventions.
5. What happened in 1851?
6. What did the 'Crystal Palace' look like?
7. How many people visited the exhibition?
8. What is telegraphy?
9. How many different goods were displayed at the exhibition?

Section B
1. What do you think a postage stamp attached to an envelope proved?
2. Why do you think only wealthy people came to the exhibition at first?
3. What do you think people thought when they saw the first telephones?
4. Why did Prince Albert decide to hold a great exhibition?
5. Why do you think the exhibition hall was described as a 'crystal palace'?
6. What does 'the ability to trade' mean?
7. Why do you think so many people came to visit 'The Great Exhibition of the Works of Industry of All Nations'?

Section C
Carefully draw and colour a picture of the 'Crystal Palace'.

The Growth of the Railways

Steam engines could pull passengers and goods very easily. This meant that poor people could travel in a way never dreamt of before. First class carriages had cushioned seats. The second class carriages had wooden benches. The third class carriages had no seats at all. New seaside resorts were built so workers from towns could travel to the coast for a treat. Also, goods made in factories could now be sold up and down the country more easily.

Copy this writing and fill in the gaps:

The Growth of the Railways

Passengers and goods could be pulled by _____ engines very easily. This meant that _____ people could travel in a way never dreamt of before. First class carriages had _____ seats. The second class carriages had _____ benches. The third class carriages had no _____ at all. Workers from towns could travel to the coast for a _____ because new seaside resorts were built. Also, goods made in _____ could now be sold more easily up and down the country.

The Growth of the Railways

The first public railway train was pulled by the 'Locomotion'. It travelled at 12 miles per hour. At the start of Victoria's reign there were only two hundred miles of railway track but by the end there were over twenty thousand!

Steam engines could pull large loads of passengers and goods very easily. This meant that poor people could travel in a way never dreamt of before.

The first railway carriages were not very comfortable. First class carriages had cushioned seats, low roofs and small windows. The second class carriages had wooden benches. The third class carriages had no seats and no roof!

All over the country new seaside resorts were built, Blackpool being one of the most famous. Workers from towns such as Blackburn or Accrington could travel to the coast for a treat. Also, goods made in factories could now be sold up and down the country more easily.

Answer these questions:

Section A
1. What was the first public railway train pulled by?
2. How fast did it travel?
3. What did steam engines pull?
4. What sort of seats were found in second class carriages?
5. What was built at the coast?
6. Why did people travel to the coast?
7. Why could goods be sold more easily?

Section B
1. What do you think it would be like to travel in a first class carriage?
2. What do you think it would be like to travel in a third class carriage?

Section C
Carefully draw and colour a picture of a steam train.

The Growth of the Railways

Twelve years before Queen Victoria came to the throne George Stephenson opened the first public railway from Stockton to Darlington. The first train was pulled by the 'Locomotion'. It travelled at 12 miles per hour. At the start of Victoria's reign there were only 200 miles of railway track but by the end there were over 20,000!

Up until this time ordinary people had travelled by foot. Stagecoaches were expensive and could only be used by wealthy people. However, steam engines could pull large loads of passengers and goods very easily. Also, the government insisted that railways must carry third class passengers for a penny a mile. This meant that poor people could travel in a way never dreamt of before.

The first railway carriages were not very comfortable. First class carriages had cushioned seats, low roofs and small windows. The second class carriages had wooden benches but the third class carriages had no seats and no roof!

All over the country new seaside resorts were built, Blackpool being one of the most famous. Workers from the Lancashire mill towns such as Blackburn or Accrington could travel to the coast for a treat. Large towns also benefitted. The goods they made in their factories could now be sold up and down the country easily, greatly increasing trade.

Answer these questions:

Section A
1 What was the first public railway train pulled by?
2 How fast did it travel?
3 What did steam engines pull?
4 What sort of seats were found in second class carriages?
5 What was built at the coast?
6 Why did people travel to the coast?
7 Why could goods be sold more easily?
8 How much railway track was built during Queen Victoria's reign?

Section B
1 What do you think it would be like to travel in a first class carriage?
2 What do you think it would be like to travel in a third class carriage?
3 How do you think people would have reacted the first time they saw a steam train pass by?
4 What does 'travel in a way never dreamt of before' mean?

Section C
Carefully draw and colour a picture of a steam train.

The Growth of the Railways

Twelve years before Queen Victoria came to the throne George Stephenson opened the first public railway from Stockton to Darlington. The first train was pulled by Stephenson's own engine, which was called the 'Locomotion'. It travelled at 12 miles per hour. A competition for new engines was held for another new railway line, which was built from Manchester to Liverpool in 1829. The winning engine was called the 'Rocket' and this could reach speeds of twenty nine miles per hour. At the start of Victoria's reign there were only 200 miles of railway track but by the end there was over 20,000!

Up until this time ordinary people had travelled everywhere by foot. Stagecoaches were expensive and could only be used by very wealthy people. Transporting goods by horse and cart along roads made mainly of earth, or mud after heavy rain, was an extremely difficult, slow and hazardous process. The invention of the railways changed all this. Steam engines running on metal rails could pull large loads of passengers and goods very easily. Also, the Government insisted that railways must carry third class passengers for a penny a mile. This meant that poor people were given the opportunity to travel in a way never dreamt of before. People in towns could travel to the seaside and back in a day.

The first railway carriages were not very comfortable. First class carriages had cushioned seats, low roofs and small windows. However, as no heating was provided, they were stuffy in summer and cold in winter. The second class carriages had wooden benches but the third class carriages had no seats and no roof. These carriages were in fact just open trucks and very uncomfortable to travel in on a cold and wet day!

All over the country new seaside resorts were built, Blackpool being one of the most famous. Workers from the Lancashire mill towns such as Blackburn or Accrington could travel to the coast for a treat. Large towns also benefitted. The goods they manufactured in their factories could now be sold up and down the country easily, greatly increasing the opportunities for trade.

Even Queen Victoria used the railways to visit her newly built homes Balmoral, which is in Scotland, and Osborne House, which is on the Isle of Wight. A new age of travel had begun.

Answer these questions:

Section A
1 What was the first public railway train pulled by?
2 How fast did it travel?
3 What did steam engines running on metal rails pull?
4 What sort of seats were found in second class carriages?
5 What was built at the coast?
6 Why did people travel to the coast?
7 Why could goods be sold more easily?
8 How much railway track was built during Queen Victoria's reign?
9 How fast did the 'Rocket' travel?

Section B
1 What do you think it would be like to travel in a first class carriage?
2 What do you think it would be like to travel in a third class carriage?
3 How do you think people would have reacted the first time they saw a steam train pass by?
4 What does 'travel in a way never dreamt of before' mean?
5 Why do you think most people travelled by foot before the railways came?
6 What do you think happened to the stagecoaches when railways had been built?
7 What is meant by the phrase 'a new age of travel'?

Section C
Carefully draw and colour a picture of a steam train.

Bicycles, Buses, Ships and Motorcars

The Penny-Farthing bicycle had a large front wheel and a small back one. In 1885 the 'Safety Bicycle' had wheels the same size and a chain. Some people travelled by horse drawn bus. Passengers could sit inside or on the roof. In 1838 paddle steamers crossed the Atlantic Ocean in only nineteen days. In 1843 the SS Great Britain was the first iron ship. In 1885 a German named Benz built the first petrol driven car. Only very wealthy people could afford the first cars.

Copy this writing and fill in the gaps:

Bicycles, Buses, Ships and Motorcars

The Penny-Farthing bicycle had a _____ front wheel and a small back one. In 1885 the '_____ Bicycle' had wheels the same size and a chain. Some people travelled by _____ drawn bus. Passengers could sit on the roof or inside. In 1838 the _____ Ocean was crossed by paddle steamers in only nineteen days. The first iron ship, the SS _____ Britain, was built in 1843. A German named _____ built the first petrol driven car in 1885. Only very _____ people could afford the first cars.

Bicycles, Buses, Ships and Motorcars

In 1868 the 'Boneshaker' bicycle had pedals fixed to the front wheel. This was followed by the Penny-Farthing, which had a huge front wheel and a tiny back one. In 1885 the 'Safety Bicycle' had wheels of equal size and a chain connected to the back wheel.

In the cities many people travelled by horse drawn bus. The first models carried the passengers inside with two extra seats by the driver. Later models also had two long benches back to back on the roof.

In 1838 paddle steamers crossed the Atlantic Ocean in nineteen days when sailing ships usually took about 33 days. In 1843 the SS Great Britain was the first ship ever to be made out of iron instead of wood.

In 1885 a German named Benz built the first petrol driven car. This was really a tricycle with a motor at the back. Two years later another German named Daimler built the first Daimler motorcar. Only very wealthy people could afford early motorcars.

Answer these questions:

Section A
1. Where did the Boneshaker bicycle have its pedals?
2. What did a Penny Farthing bicycle look like?
3. What was invented in 1885?
4. How did many people travel in the cities?
5. Where did the passengers sit in a horse drawn bus?
6. Which was the first ship to be made from iron?
7. Who built the first petrol driven car?

Section B
1. What do you think it would be like to ride on a Penny Farthing?
2. Which bicycle looked similar to a modern bicycle? Give reasons for your answer.

Section C
Carefully draw and colour a picture of a Penny Farthing.

Bicycles, Buses, Ships and Motorcars

The 'Boneshaker' bicycle had no chain as the pedals were fixed to the front wheel. This was followed by the Penny-Farthing, which had a huge front wheel and a tiny back one. In 1885 the 'Safety Bicycle' had wheels of equal size and a chain connected to the back wheel.

In the cities many people travelled by horse drawn bus. The first models carried the passengers inside with two extra seats by the driver. Later models also had two long benches back to back on the roof.

In 1838 paddle steamers crossed the Atlantic Ocean in nineteen days when sailing ships usually took about 33 days. In 1843 the SS Great Britain was the first ship ever to be made out of iron instead of wood. Wind powered 'Clippers' were faster than almost any steam ship afloat. They were used to carry tea from China and wool from Australia.

The very first 'horseless carriages' were powered by steam and were very slow. In 1885 a German named Benz built the first petrol driven car. This was really a tricycle with a motor at the back. Two years later another German named Daimler built the first Daimler motorcar. Both men had found the advantage of petrol over steam was that the engine could be much smaller and lighter. Only very wealthy people could afford early motorcars.

Answer these questions:

Section A
1. Where did the Boneshaker bicycle have its pedals?
2. What did a Penny Farthing bicycle look like?
3. What was invented in 1885?
4. How did many people travel in the cities?
5. Where did the passengers sit in a horse drawn bus?
6. Which was the first ship to be made from iron?
7. Who built the first petrol driven car?
8. What were wind powered 'Clippers' used for?

Section B
1. What do you think it would be like to ride on a Penny Farthing?
2. Which bicycle looked similar to a modern bicycle? Give reasons for your answer.
3. Why do you think the steam ships were quicker than sailing ships crossing the Atlantic Ocean?
4. Why do you think only wealthy people owned cars?

Section C
Carefully draw and colour a picture of a Penny Farthing.

Bicycles, Buses, Ships and Motorcars

In 1868 the 'Boneshaker' bicycle was invented. It had no chain as the pedals were fixed to the front wheel. When you went downhill the pedals whizzed round so fast you had to take your feet off! This was followed by the Penny-Farthing, which had a huge front wheel and a tiny back one. The rider sat nearly 2 metres above the ground. Penny-Farthings could go at some speed but at times were very dangerous and the rider had a long way to fall if they crashed! In 1885 the 'Safety Bicycle' was invented. This had wheels of equal size and a chain connected to the back wheel. At first they had solid rubber tyres which were very hard but three years later Dunlop invented air filled tyres which made for a much more comfortable ride.

In the towns and cities many people travelled by horse drawn bus. The first models carried the passengers inside with two extra seats by the driver. Later models also had two long benches back to back on the roof. Only men were allowed on top since ladies could not be expected to climb the iron ladder in their long trailing skirts.

In 1838 the paddle steamers 'Sirius' and 'Great Western' crossed the Atlantic Ocean in nineteen days when sailing ships usually took about 33 days. In 1843 the SS Great Britain was the first ship ever to be made out of iron instead of wood. When it was launched it was the largest vessel afloat. Its first voyage across the Atlantic took only 14 days, another record for a steam powered ship. Although steam ships were getting faster, the wind powered 'Clippers', were faster than almost any steam ship afloat. They were used to carry tea from China and wool from Australia right up until 1869 when the Suez Canal was opened. This created a much shorter route but could only be used by steam powered ships.

The very first 'horseless carriages' were powered by steam and were very heavy and slow. They were considered so dangerous that a law was passed in 1862 insisting a man had to walk in front of vehicles carrying a red flag. In 1885 a German named Benz built the first petrol driven car. This was really a tricycle with a motor at the back. Two years later another German named Daimler built the first Daimler motorcar. Both men had found the advantage of petrol over steam was that the engine could be much smaller and lighter. When the first petrol cars were seen, the government were persuaded to abolish the red flag law in 1896. Only very wealthy people could afford early motorcars.

Answer these questions:

Section A
1. Where did the Boneshaker bicycle have its pedals?
2. What did a Penny Farthing bicycle look like?
3. What was invented in 1885?
4. How did many people travel in the cities?
5. Where did the passengers sit in a horse drawn bus?
6. Which was the first ship to be made from iron?
7. Who built the first petrol driven car?
8. What were wind powered 'Clippers' used for?
9. Why was a new law passed in 1862?

Section B
1. What do you think it would be like to ride on a Penny Farthing?
2. Which bicycle looked similar to a modern bicycle? Give reasons for your answer.
3. Why do you think the steam ships were quicker than sailing ships crossing the Atlantic Ocean?
4. Why do you think only wealthy people owned cars?
5. What difference did Dunlop's invention make to cycling?
6. How do you think ordinary people felt about the red flag law?
7. What is a 'horseless carriage'?

Section C
Carefully draw and colour a picture of a Penny Farthing.

Victorian Fashion

Women's Fashion: At the beginning of Victoria's reign ladies wore five or six petticoats under long dresses with tiny waists. Later the bustle became popular. This was a pad or cushion worn to make a lady's skirt stand out behind.

Men's Fashion: At the beginning of Victoria's reign men wore a neck-cloth tied in a knot. Almost every Victorian gentleman wore a moustache. Later on, side whiskers became popular. Towards the end of Victoria's reign matching jackets and trousers were popular worn with a shirt and tie.

Copy this writing and fill in the gaps:

Victorian Fashion

Ladies wore five or six _____ under long dresses with tiny waists at the beginning of Victoria's reign. The _____ became popular later. This was a cushion or pad worn to make a lady's skirt _____ out behind. Men wore a neck-cloth tied in a _____ at the beginning of Victoria's reign. A _____ was worn by almost every Victorian gentleman. Later on, side _____ became popular. Towards the end of Victoria's reign matching jackets and _____ were popular worn with a shirt and tie.

Victorian Fashion

Women's Fashion: At the beginning of Victoria's reign, ladies wore five or six petticoats under dresses of silk and taffeta. Skirts and dresses went down to the floor. Tiny waists were fashionable. Dresses for dances or balls were low-cut and showed off bare shoulders.

Later the bustle became fashionable. This was a pad or cushion worn at the back, just below the waistline, to make a lady's skirt stand out behind. Towards the end of Victoria's reign, dresses with 'leg-of-mutton' sleeves accompanied by muffs and fans were popular.

Men's Fashion: At the beginning of Victoria's reign, men wore a neck-cloth tied in a knot instead of a collar and tie. Almost every Victorian gentleman wore a moustache. Later on side whiskers became popular.

Towards the end of Victoria's reign, suits were popular worn with a shirt and tie. Top hats and bowler hats were popular. Flat caps were often worn by less well off men.

Answer these questions:

Section A
1. How many petticoats did ladies wear?
2. How long were skirts and dresses?
3. What is a bustle?
4. What did ladies wear at the end of Victoria's reign?
5. What did men wear round their necks at first?
6. What did men wear on their faces?
7. What were suits worn with?

Section B
1. Why do you think women wore so many petticoats?
2. Why do you think flat caps were worn by less well off men?

Section C
Carefully draw and colour a picture of a man and a woman wearing Victorian clothes.

Victorian Fashion

Women's Fashion

At the beginning of Victoria's reign, ladies wore many clothes. They would often wear five or six petticoats under dresses of silk and taffeta. Skirts and dresses went down to the floor. Tiny waists were fashionable. Dresses for dances or balls were low-cut and exposed bare shoulders. In the middle of Victoria's reign came the crinoline, a full-hooped petticoat, which expanded the skirt worn over it. Later the bustle became fashionable. This was a pad or cushion worn at the back, just below the waistline, to make a lady's skirt stand out behind. Towards the end of Victoria's reign, dresses with 'leg-of-mutton' sleeves (a loose, full sleeve that's rounded from the shoulder to below the elbow, then shaped to the arm) accompanied by muffs and fans were popular.

Men's Fashion

At the beginning of Victoria's reign, men wore a neck-cloth tied in a knot instead of a collar and tie. Almost every Victorian gentleman wore a moustache. Later on beards became popular along with smoking cigarettes. (Victorian men did not understand that smoking would damage their health!) Towards the end of Victoria's reign, suits were popular worn with a shirt and tie. Top hats (a tall hat usually covered with silk) and bowler hats (a felt hat that is round and hard with a narrow brim) were popular. Flat caps were often worn by less well off men.

Answer these questions:

Section A
1 How many petticoats did ladies wear?
2 How long were skirts and dresses?
3 What is a bustle?
4 What did ladies wear at the end of Victoria's reign?
5 What did men wear round their necks at first?
6 What did men wear on their faces?
7 What were suits worn with?
8 Who wore flat caps?

Section B
1 Why do you think women wore so many petticoats?
2 What is the difference between a top hat and a bowler hat?
3 Describe a 'leg-of-mutton' sleeve.
4 Why do you think Victorian men did not understand the dangers of smoking?

Section C
Carefully draw and colour a picture of a man and a woman wearing Victorian clothes.

Victorian Fashion

Queen Victoria was on the throne for 64 years, having reigned longer than any other English monarch. There were many changes of fashion during this period.

Women's Fashion
At the beginning of Victoria's reign, ladies wore a great many clothes. They would often wear five or six petticoats under dresses of silk and taffeta. Skirts and dresses went down to the floor. Tiny waists were fashionable. Women would wear a corset (a tight fitting garment to shape the body) so tightly laced up they could possibly faint! Poke bonnets (a hat in the shape of a hood which would shade the face of the wearer) and shawls were fashionable. Dresses for dances or balls were low-cut exposing bare shoulders.

In the middle of the reign came the crinoline, a full-hooped petticoat, which expanded the skirt worn over it. Later the bustle became fashionable. This was a pad or cushion worn at the back, just below the waistline, to make a lady's skirt stand out behind. Towards the end of Victoria's reign, dresses with 'leg-of-mutton' sleeves (a loose, full sleeve that's rounded from the shoulder to below the elbow, then shaped to the arm) accompanied by muffs and fans were popular. Sportswear for women such as bicycling dresses, tennis dresses and swimwear also became popular.

Men's Fashion
At the beginning of Victoria's reign, men wore a neck-cloth tied in a knot instead of a collar and tie. Almost every Victorian gentleman wore a moustache although some preferred side-whiskers called mutton-chops. Later on beards became popular along with smoking cigarettes. (Victorian men did not understand that smoking would damage their health!)

Towards the end of Victoria's reign, men's clothes became similar to those worn in the twentieth century. Suits were popular, worn with a shirt and tie. Top hats (a tall hat usually covered with silk) and bowler hats (a felt hat that is round and hard with a narrow brim) were popular. Straw boaters (a kind of hat associated with sailing) were fashionable in the summer. Flat caps were often worn by less well off men.

Answer these questions:

Section A
1. How many petticoats did ladies wear?
2. How long were skirts and dresses?
3. What is a bustle?
4. What did ladies wear at the end of Victoria's reign?
5. What did men wear round their necks at first?
6. What did men wear on their faces?
7. What were suits worn with?
8. Who wore flat caps?
9. When were straw boaters worn?

Section B
1. Why do you think women wore so many petticoats?
2. What is the difference between a top hat and a bowler hat?
3. Describe a 'leg-of-mutton' sleeve.
4. Why do you think Victorian men did not understand the dangers of smoking?
5. Why were some women in danger of fainting?
6. Why do you think women wore different clothes when doing sport?
7. What is a 'neck cloth'?

Section C
Carefully draw and colour a picture of a man and a woman wearing Victorian clothes.

The British Empire

An Empire is built when one country rules over a

number of others. British explorers discovered

and claimed new countries for the British Empire.

They included Canada, parts of America, parts of

Africa, India, Australia and New Zealand. Once a

new country was discovered, traders, soldiers and

priests were sent to set up trading posts to buy

local raw materials such as gold, fur, spices and

diamonds. The British Empire no longer exists,

but since then, many people from other countries

have come to live in Britain.

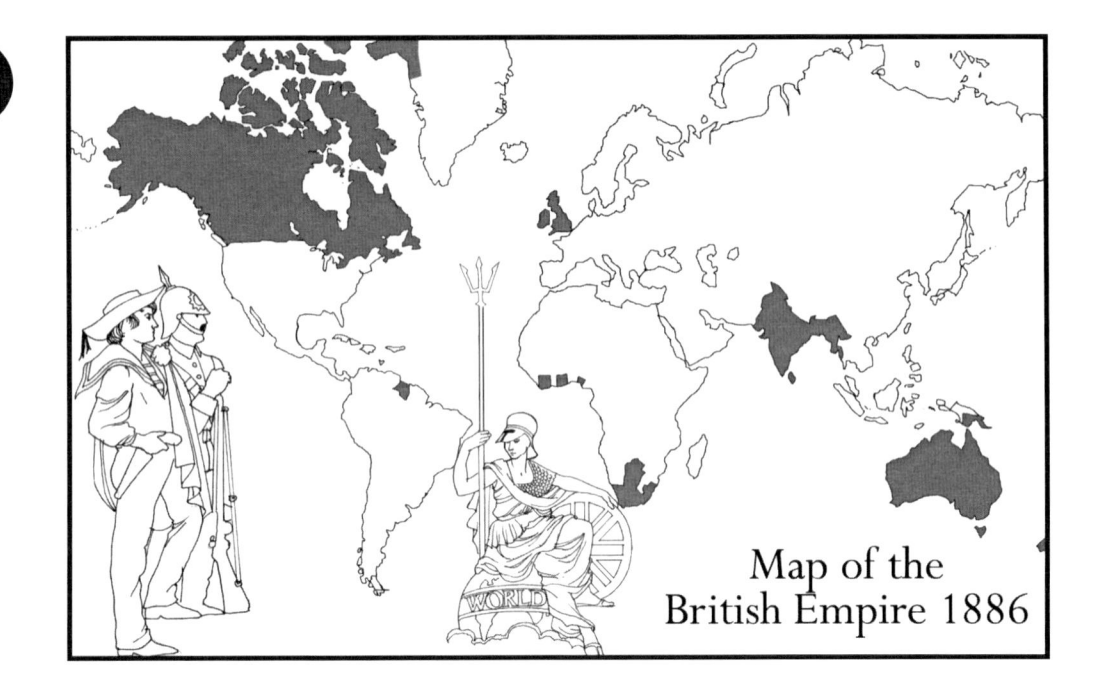

Map of the
British Empire 1886

Copy this writing and fill in the gaps:

The British Empire
An Empire is built when one _____ rules over a number of others. British _____ discovered and claimed new countries for the _____ Empire. They included Australia, New _____, Canada, parts of America, parts of Africa and India. Once a new country was discovered, _____, priests and traders, were sent to set up trading posts to buy local raw materials such as_____, gold, spices and fur. The _____ Empire no longer exists, but since then, many people from other countries have come to live in Britain.

The British Empire

An Empire is built when one country rules over a number of others. Captain Cook discovered and claimed Australia and New Zealand. As each new country was discovered, the size of the British Empire grew.

The British Empire included Canada, parts of America, parts of Africa, India, Australia, New Zealand and a number of other smaller countries. They were called the British overseas colonies.

Once a new country was discovered, traders, soldiers and priests were sent to set up safe trading posts. Cheap local labour would be used and trade started in local raw materials such as gold, fur, diamonds, spices etc.

The British Empire no longer exists. Since the Second World War most former colonies have become self-governing countries. Over time, many people from the colonies came to live in Britain. This is how Britain became a multicultural society.

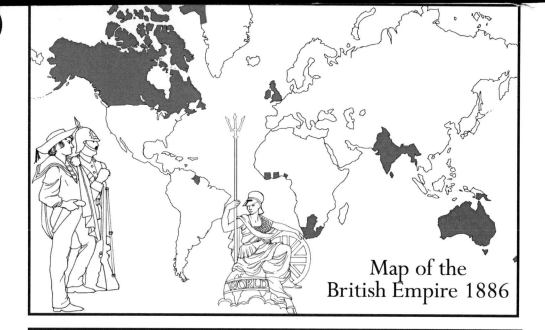

Map of the British Empire 1886

Answer these questions:

Section A
1. What is an Empire?
2. What did Captain Cook discover?
3. Which countries were in the British Empire?
4. Who was sent to set up trading posts?
5. What sort of materials were traded?
6. Does the British Empire still exist?
7. How did Britain become a multicultural society?

Section B
1. What is a 'trading post'?
2. What is a multicultural society?

Section C
Carefully draw and colour a simple map of the British Empire.

The British Empire

An Empire is built when one country rules over a number of others. Columbus, a Spaniard, discovered and claimed Central America. Cook, an Englishman, discovered and claimed Australia and New Zealand. As each new country was discovered, the European countries made claims to these distant lands, increasing the size of their Empires.

The British Empire became the largest of the European Empires. It consisted of what is now known as Canada, parts of America, parts of Africa, India, Australia, New Zealand and a number of other smaller countries. They were called the British overseas colonies.

These colonies were established by taking over areas that were already settled. Once discovered, traders, soldiers and priests were sent to set up safe trading posts. Cheap local labour would be used and trade started in local raw materials such as gold, fur, diamonds, spices etc.

The British Empire no longer exists. Since the Second World War most former colonies have become self-governing countries. The Commonwealth is the name given to the collection of countries that used to be part of the British Empire. Many people from the Commonwealth countries and their descendents now live in Britain. This is how Britain became a multicultural society.

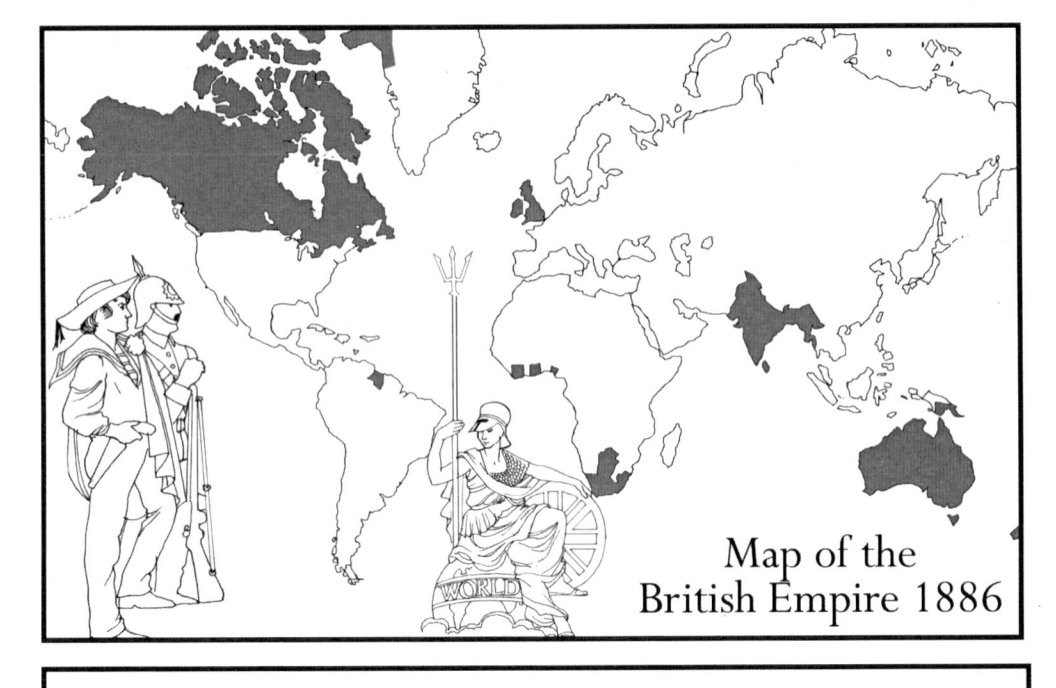

Map of the
British Empire 1886

Answer these questions:

Section A
1 What is an Empire?
2 What did Captain Cook discover?
3 Which countries were in the British Empire?
4 Who was sent to set up trading posts?
5 What sort of materials were traded?
6 Does the British Empire still exist?
7 How did Britain become a multicultural society?
8 What is the Commonwealth?

Section B
1 What do you think a 'trading post' is?
2 What is a multicultural society?
3 What was a 'British overseas colony'?
4 How do you think the people of an African country would feel about being taken over by Victorian Britain?

Section C
Carefully draw and colour a simple map of the British Empire.